Journey into Simple Living

Journey into Simple Living

SELF-CARE PRACTICES FOR BUSY WOMEN

Annie Singh-Quern

COA Consulting, LLC

Published by COA Consulting, LLC
coaconsultingservices.com

Journey into Simple Living. SELF-CARE PRACTICES FOR BUSY WOMEN.

Copyright© 2020 by Annie Singh-Quern

Note: This book does not replace the advice of a medical
professional or counselor. The author and publisher do not
assume any liability for loss, damage, and risk - personal or otherwise,
directly or indirectly - caused by errors, omissions, inclusions,
use, and application of any content of this book.
For information, contact the publisher at www.coaconsultingservices.com

Paperback
ISBN: 978-1-7360737-0-4

Design by Vicki Sanders, vwahlacreative, LLC
Author Photograph by Dana Scott, DMS Creative Solutions, LLC

Printed by Kindle Direct Publishing, U.S.A.

Dedication

In memory of our beloved Roy, without whom
this project would not be possible.

For my children, Olivia and Connor, who inspire
me every day to live my best life.

And to all those women who are courageous enough
to embark on the journey of a simple life.

*The dove in flight symbolizes the simple living journey
for joy, meaning, and peace. The heart signifies self-care;
the vine denotes our bond with nature.*

Contents

Introduction

To You

If you are a busy woman who yearns deeply for tranquility and peace in our fast-paced world, then this book is for you. The compilation of 75 easy practices, reflective exercises, and resources was designed to help bring simplicity and serenity to your hours, days, and ultimately, to your life.

I hope you will allow me to escort you along the way.

Best,

Annie

Why the Simple Life?

The simple life eludes so many of us. As busy women, we are bombarded daily by forces that threaten to pull us away from our core selves.

We're consumed with our numerous roles as moms, wives, daughters, siblings, friends, employers, and colleagues.

Our schedules burgeon with meetings, phone calls, texts, social media, television, social gatherings, school activities, housework, and errands.

We shove and stuff the "must-dos" into a 24-hour day until there is barely any room for "me."

This cycle repeats and rolls into weeks, months, years, and before we realize it, decades.

Over time, this kind of living can tax our bodies, minds, hearts, and souls. Apart from the mental, physical, and emotional ramifications of living a hectic life, we've been robbed of the precious gift of time.

How can we use and cherish the time we've been given, the time we have left? The answer is to live simply.

The Simple Life is about savoring every moment gifted to us. To begin to live a simple life, we must first *choose* to live simply. Then, we must take small, intentional steps to create habits that form a lifestyle.

Leading a simple life gives us more time for ourselves and with our loved ones. It also makes our time here on earth more meaningful and peaceful.

How to Get the Most Out of this Book

There are four main components in this book that cater to your simple living journey:

- Recommended practices in simple living - e.g., creating a sacred space, dining by candlelight, and reading daily.

- Personal reflective exercises - e.g., findings from a nature walk, favorite "feel-good" books, and a sketch for a simple summer garden.

- A weekly calendar to track daily activities.

- A self-care vision board for planning ahead and staying centered.

To get the most out of this book, try all of the suggested activities. Some or all may resonate with you. All the practices can be attained in and around your home. However, the exercises may require an ounce of dedication and patience, a relatively small price to pay for living a fulfilling and peaceful life.

To begin your journey to simple living, take inventory of your current activities for about a week, then reflect on them. Are there activities that drain you, ones that you follow on impulse that don't provide a sense of purpose and peace? Try putting those negative activities aside, one by one, to make room for some or all of the recommended practices. You can slot in a task or move parts of your day around to accommodate the activity. The next day, add a new exercise, but try to continue the first one in your schedule for at least a week.

For a month, keep track of your activities in the simple calendar at the back of the book. See how the practices fit in naturally with your life. Over time, the steps to lead a simple life will become habitual and start flooding your schedule. Because they come from a happy, nurturing place, these exercises should gently fill your days, weeks, months, years, and, ultimately, your life.

My Story

My childhood days were seeped in simplicity and serenity. They included playing hide-and-seek with friends, reading quietly with my mom, and comfortably sharing a chair with my brother, Roy, to watch our dad hand-stir the batter for the annual Christmas cake our mom baked for family and friends. Those days were, by far, the best days of my young life - creating memories in the simplest way possible. These precious times became the foundation of this book.

Then came my tumultuous 20's. Fresh out of college, I stumbled to find the meaning of life. I was like a spinning top, an endless cycle of twirling with no real direction. Serial dating, fast cars, shopping, and living paycheck-to-paycheck, were a few of the many self-limiting habits of a young, lost adult. I had begun a descent into the harried life.

The third stage of my life came when I moved to live overseas in 2000; newly married and fresh in the world of expatriate living. Seeking immediate gratification continued with exotic trips, shopping sprees, and weekend parties.

At 36, I became a mother for the first time. Ironically, I began to find meaning by caring for my daughter. My appetite for craving for more began to wane. The top was slowing down. I started to gain glimpses of the real me.

I met my beautiful friend, Carol, when my daughter, Olivia, was two years old. As a young mother who had just lost her husband to cancer, Carol was determined to live life to the fullest. Our friendship days were carefree and full of laughter, watching our kids grow up - until her diagnosis. Stage 3 uterine cancer required immediate and aggressive treatment.

Three years later, following many rounds of chemotherapy and countless days in bed, Carol shared that she did not have much time left. "I'm leaving the city," she said. Far away from a world that was noisy and uncertain, she sought serenity and simplicity. Unfortunately, we lost Carol just two months after my son, Connor, was born. My friend Carol became the second inspiration for this book.

The fourth stage of my life is now, as a single parent in my 50's. Losing my brother suddenly this past summer, in the middle of the Coronavirus pandemic, has put the emergency brake on my life. I reached for ways to journey inside of myself, seeking simplicity and serenity in my surroundings. Wandering the wooded paths in my neighborhood at dawn and dusk brought me close to moments of magic. Black ink etched in the veins of leaves, the incessant cry of cicadas, the lingering scent of magnolia, and the brush of pink in the awakening sky are some of the beauty I've come to know, all meshed with the pain of recently losing my best friend.

The sharp realization is that the end is closer than the beginning. How would I like to live the rest of the years? All I need is right in front of me and within me. The top has stopped spinning. I am now left with the choice to treasure the gift of time.

I invite you to come along on the journey to discover a beautiful, simple life, and you.

Pledge

I have one precious life.

I deserve to live it from my inner self, my core.

Living life from my core allows me to experience deserving joy, meaning, and peace.

I will connect to my inner self by caring for me.

I will care for my inner self through simple, daily practices that are seeped in simplicity and serenity.

Engaging in a lifestyle of self-care soaked in simplicity and serenity is called simple living.

Living simply will bring a sense of joy, meaning, and peace to my life.

Simple Living will also allow me to cherish the gift of time.

A simple living lifestyle will make my life more whole, more me, and more free.

I will take the simple steps to self-care because I deserve to live a life of joy, meaning, and peace.

_____

Name

_____

Signature   Date

*"Self-care is a sacred journey of
honoring our bodies, hearts, and souls."*

— Annie Singh-Quern

SELF-CARE PRACTICES, REFLECTIONS AND RESOURCES

Morning

Sit with the Sun

Do you get up early enough to watch the sun rise? Do you remember the hushed darkness, the walk to the window, and the first brush of color in the sky?

Leave the house and find a spot to sit outside, facing the east. Arrive just before the faintest color begins to seep into the sky. Breathe in the little night air that's left. Soak in the silence.

Transfix your eyes to the magic show. Indulge as if you're creating a painting, step-by-step, for the very first time. Follow the hues as they slowly take shape on the canvas. Does soft yellow fold into brilliant gold before melting into the light of the day?

Is the skittish squirrel oblivious to the awakening? Are the leaves twinkling in the sliver of rays? Are Robins sipping the last of the morning dew?

Sit and look. You may have just about 30 sacred minutes before light blankets the night and another day churns in motion.

Sunrise

(Memorable sunrise experience.)

Beautiful Bed

You will probably spend one-third of your life sleeping, and most often, it will be in your bed. Your bed is more than a physical place; it's a place to relax and heal. Care for your bed by dedicating some time to make it.

Making your bed each morning will take less than ten minutes. At the end of the day, you'll be eager to climb back into your resting place because it looks and feels inviting.

First, remove the pillows, one by one, and support them on a nearby chair. Then, straighten the fitted and flat sheets and tuck them neatly under the mattress.

Fluff up each pillow (adorn your bed with as many pillows as your heart desires) before repositioning them at the headboard.

Using the palm of your hands, gently straighten out any remaining creases on the bed.

Finally, lightly spray your favorite scent over your beautiful bed, or tuck a scented sachet under your pillow.

A Beautiful Bed

"After my maternal grandfather passed away, I began to pay more visits to my grandmother. Sometimes, I would catch her right after her afternoon nap. She'd be making her bed.

My granny spent time tending to her bed as though she had all the time in the world. For her, it was a ritual rather than a chore. Hand-embroidered pillows lay side-by-side, as though gramps was saving a spot for grandfather. Finally, Grandma draped her favorite ivory throw that she had crocheted some twenty years before.

Usually, I helped my grandmother make her beautiful bed; sometimes I was content to watch her. In the end, she would motion me to sit where my grandfather used to rest. And, grandma would take a seat on her side, and we would chat."

— Annie Singh-Quern

Breathe

Just before you get out of bed, practice some deep breathing.

Close your eyes. Inhale deeply, through your nose. Feel the coolness of your breath as it enters your nostrils. Your chest will expand as the air fills your lungs.

Hold your breath by counting slowly, "1, 2, 3."

Then, exhale the now-cool air, in one full stream, through pursed lips.

Repeat two more times.

This mindful exercise will place oxygen deep into your lungs and cells for breathing and healthy living.

Meaningful Mantras

Mantras are powerful words that allow us to connect to a level of centeredness. Make them a part of your day when you feel a need to be more focused.

Choose a single word or a string of words that is positive, simple, easy to say and has meaning in your life. It could be "Blessed" or "My life is full."

Mantras can be said quietly, under your breath, or silently.

You can use your mantra when you are sitting in traffic, trying to relax before a meeting, or even if you are feeling anxious.

Mantras

_____

_____

_____

_____

_____

_____

_____

_____

_____

_____

_____

(Simple, positive, and meaningful words.)

Wander

Being around Mother Nature is calming and healing.

Turn your phone off, put it away, or place it deep in your pocket.

Begin walking by taking slow, light steps. Interchange them for heavier ones with your heels pressed firmly into the ground.

If the ground is level, stable, and safe, walk barefoot. Feel the soft grass against the padding of your soles. Look down and study how the grass has taken shape around your feet.

Walk in the sunlight and shade, at dawn and dusk, and in the warm rain (without thunder and lighting).

Engage all five of your senses: cast your gaze above towering trees, inhale the heady scent of magnolias, seek the velvet touch of a new leaf, and steal a glimpse of a Cardinal anxious for flight. If you come across running water, stop, and listen to its gurgling. Watch it flow over rocks and take nature's gifts along for a ride.

Stop - listen, look, smell, taste, touch. Then, stop, again.

Make your walk at least 45 minutes daily.

Nature Walk

(Engage all senses during your stroll.)

Nature Walk Souvenirs

(Place your keepsakes, with notes, here.)

Say "Hello"

Sit down and handwrite a note to someone you care about. It can be a letter to a friend to say "hi," an expression of gratitude, or an invite.

Think about the letters you've saved from loved ones. What made the notes special enough for your keepsake box? Was it the beautifully designed stationery, the elegant handwriting, the message itself, or all of it?

Think of the note you're about to write not just as words on a piece of paper, but as a gift. For the letter, choose paper with plain lines, elaborate designs, or color.

Pull up your favorite chair at home or sit on a bench in your garden to write. Enjoy a cup of tea while you are at your task.

Use a colored pen, simple black ink, or a fancy fountain pen. Try your best handwriting. Use cursive. Form each letter carefully, slowly, and neatly.

Address the envelope with care, taking your time to center the words. Dress your letter with specially-designed postage stamps.

Send the letter off and picture the sweet surprise of the receiver.

Now, sit down to write a note to yourself.

Letter to Self

_____

_____

_____

_____

_____

_____

_____

_____

_____

_____

_____

_____

(A note to your past, present, or future self.)

Afternoon

Pack a Picnic

You don't always have to sit at the dining room table to eat a meal. For a change of scenery, venture outdoors for a picnic, alone or with loved ones. You can escape to your backyard or a neighborhood park.

Try lunch, mid-afternoon snack, or early dinner. Pack a picnic basket with all your favorite items and head to your picnic site.

Decide on your scenery. Is it the red and white tulips in your garden, the wooded path across your back porch, or a grassy patch where the kids are playing ball.

Lay the picnic tablecloth and set out your food and other items. For a centerpiece, arrange some fragrant flowers in a makeshift vase or place sprigs of fresh herbs beside your napkin.

For added relaxation, open a book, or just rest on your back and close your eyes.

Picnic Basket

Pack and store a picnic basket in your pantry.
When you're ready for a picnic adventure, you'll be
prepared to go. Just add your edibles. After your picnic,
quickly refresh the basket with non-perishable items.

- Tablecloth (waterproof)

- Homemade snacks & water

- Paper plates, cups, utensils & napkins

- Book, notebook & pen

- Hat & shades

- A makeshift vase (a tin or a cup
  for holding wildflowers)

- Candles & matches

- Small first aid kit & sunscreen

- Trash bag

Garden for Goodies

There is something satisfying about eating the produce you raise; a sense of pride and accomplishment, beyond knowing the origins of your food.

You don't need a big back yard or an elaborate setup to plant your own vegetables. Carve out a small area in your yard. It could be your back porch, with just the right amount of shade and sun.

Gather easy gardening tips and tools from your neighborhood nursery. Spend time choosing the soil, the seeds, and the saplings. Get ready to garden with a hat, your gloves, and your plants.

Do you enjoy salads? You can plant cucumbers, tomatoes, and peppers. If you lack space, then place some individual pots on your deck. Not enough space or even time? Stick some herbs in colorful containers at your kitchen window. They will make the place smell fresh and also be readily available to add to your dishes.

Don't be shy about becoming messy when you garden. It's more fun when you dig in!

Flowers, Vegetables & Herbs

(Favorites for viewing, planting, and eating.)

Glorious Garden

(Design your dream garden to plant your favorite goodies.)

Learn at the Library

Neighborhood libraries are great places to learn, relax, and get away from the hustle and bustle of the day. Members may speak in hushed tones and whispers while others remain quiet, reading, browsing, and studying.

At the library, go on a hunt in your favorite book section or try a new area of interest. If it's language, explore the many ways of greeting in French, German, or Arabic. Select an autobiography of a famous person or a collection of lovely verses crafted by your favorite poet.

Find a favorite spot to sit: by the window, at a communal table, or in the reference section. Savor the hush. Lose yourself in a world of words.

Visit the library once a week.

Topics & Titles

_____

_____

_____

_____

_____

_____

_____

_____

_____

_____

_____

_____

(Explore a present or new interest.)

Library Days

"Visiting the library has always been a treat to me. As a little girl, I would hop on the padded crossbars of my dad's bicycle to the library. I always felt safe with my dad's arms around me and his lingering scent of Old Spice as he pedaled along the road streaming with cars and trucks.

The library was a small, one-story concrete building. Sometimes, a night of torrential pour would flood the ground, leaving us to walk a narrow plank to the front door. Most of the books carried dog ears, but I was happy just to discover a new read. I stayed lost in my little world until my dad came to find me.

A librarian would help my dad choose another romance for my mom and issue a ticket stamped with the due date. We'd gather our books, and I would climb on the bike again to make our way along the busy road. I couldn't wait to show my mom her new book and dig into mine."

— Annie Singh-Quern

Foraging Finds

Foraging provides an exploration for all good and edible things that nature has blessed us with here on earth. It also gives us a chance to appreciate the surprising beauty around us.

Choose a spot to forage. It could be right in your yard. You may find treasures such as sprigs of wild onion, delicious blackberries, and edible flowers like dandelions to add to your next meal.

Gain deeper knowledge about foraging by reading extensively and seeking insights from a local foraging expert.

"I love how I can just call a few girlfriends over for an impromptu potluck and we can make a truly memorable night out of it."

— Annie Singh-Quern

Potluck Party

Planning a potluck can be a stress-free and guilt-free affair with friends and family. One of the cool things about this kind of gathering is that you can enjoy different dishes with your favorite people without doing much work.

The first step in planning a potluck is to decide on your guest list, a fun theme, and a time of the day that works well for all of you.

Fun themes can be Superfoods, Mediterranean Cuisine, or a Hawaiian Luau during the summer. The party can be held inside or in your garden. As the hostess, you can make the main course and leave it up to your guests to bring the side dishes.

Hosting a potluck could be spontaneous. Just call a small group of girlfriends over to share leftovers or appetizers. Have fun and make memories.

Plan a Potluck

Theme

_____

_____

_____

Guest list

_____

_____

_____

_____

_____

_____

Helpful Hands

Our hands are miraculous inventions. We use them to turn the faucet on, stroke the skin of our loved ones, and spoon food into our mouths. It's only fair that we take good care of our hands.

Have you ever spent time touching every inch of your fingers: pressing, squeezing, and rubbing? Have you noticed the faint and deep lines on your palm - the ones that crisscross and disappear to the back of your hand? If someone were to make imprints of your palms, would you be able to identify which ones belong to you?

One easy way to care for your hands is to massage them:

- Squeeze a dime-size lotion into your palm.
- Rub the liquid into the insides of your hands, using a circular motion.
- Smooth the lotion on the back of your hand.
- Circle your wrist and travel back to your palm.
- Knead the palm of your hand with your thumb.
- Switch hands.
- End the massage in a clasp, gently pressing your hands together.

Carve out time to care for your hands on a daily basis.

Marvelous Mani

"When I was a little girl, my mom spent part of her Sundays giving herself a manicure. It was usually in the afternoon after the lunch dishes were washed. Tending to her nails was my mother's little way of caring for herself while enjoying quiet time away from the brood.

I always brought the manicure kit to the dining room table where mom sat patiently waiting. She carefully removed the polish using a single cotton pad for each hand. Next, she filed her nails ending in a perfectly round tip. She gave herself only three choices of nail polish: clear, taupe, and blush-pink. She never seemed to miss the mark with the polish.

As young as I was, I admired my mother's fingers - long and slender, and always working for us, except on Sunday afternoons."

— Annie Singh-Quern

Give Back

Giving back connects us not only to those we help but to ourselves. When we help improve the lives of those in need, we are nurtured in return.

We give back to individuals and groups in need to which we feel connected. The mission of an organization and the values for which it stands may resonate within us. Have you overcome a challenge and are now seeking a cause where you can share your assets? You'll be motivating others through your empowerment, and vise versa.

Quietly ask yourself why you choose to support one cause over another, knowing that they are all worthy in their unique ways. Then choose a way to give back, based on your passion, availability, skills, and expertise. You may provide support through a monetary donation or volunteer your time and effort.

Explore the needs in your community and match them with the calling of your heart.

Nonprofits & Causes

(Local missions that move you.)

Every Day

Sweet Sanctuary

Every woman should have a sacred space in her home where she can feel safe and free to connect to her inner self. This quiet spot or sanctuary allows you to relax, reflect, reminisce, and ultimately recharge to face daily living in a calm and centered manner. In your sacred space, you'll be able to reflect on your thoughts, emotions, and feelings without judgment. This is your space; it belongs to you and only you.

A sacred space can be present in any part of your home as long as it's a private spot away from traffic and noise. Explore a nook, your bed, an armchair, or a room.

Indulge the five senses when preparing your sweet sanctuary:

Sight: An inspirational quote in a beautiful frame.

Touch: A throw adds warmth and comfort during reflection.

Sound: Soft music will lull you into a tranquil state.

Smell: Candles create the perfect relaxation mood.

Taste: A cup of warm caffeine-free tea is soothing.

Schedule time in your calendar for solitude in your sacred space.

My Sacred Space

Where:

Sight:

Touch:

Sound:

Smell:

Taste:

Time:

Relish Reading

Carve out a time to read each day. It could be just when you wake up, after lunch, or just before bedtime.

Choose any book, fiction or nonfiction. (Magazines may not lend enough time for one to be fully immersed in a topic.) Explore a new topic or deepen your knowledge of a familiar one.

Try your best to stay away from distractions. If you are reading outside, choose a quiet spot without much foot traffic. Turn your electronics off.

Read in your bed, in your favorite chair, by the window, out in your garden, or on a park bench. Before you know it, time will slip away from you.

Mark your pages with a pressed leaf from a walk, a favorite photo of your loved one, or a braided ribbon from a craft activity.

Expand your reading experience by joining a book club or creating one with like-minded people.

Read for at least 30 minutes a day.

Book Club

_____

_____

_____

_____

_____

_____

_____

_____

_____

_____

_____

(Create a book club: name, members, meeting place, etc.)

Prose & Poem

(Quotes and verses that speak to you.)

*"The difference between a good book
and a great book is that with a good book,
time seems to speed by; with a great book,
you wish it wouldn't.*

— Annie Singh-Quern

Go Wild with Water

We've all heard it. "Our bodies are made up of at least 60% water. Water is the fountain of life. We should consume eight glasses a day." So, drink water!

Don't wait to feel thirsty to have a drink. Just pour yourself a glass and keep it close to you. Every time you look up from your task, take a drink, or when you walk by the desk, reach down and pick up the cup.

To add a punch to your water, experiment with natural flavors. Add fruit, herb, or vegetable - a sprig of mint that you're growing by your windowsill, a generous squeeze of fresh lemon from a local farm, sliced strawberries or cucumbers off your garden plants, or for extra zest, a dash of cayenne pepper.

Try room temperature, warm, or cold water.

Savor "the fountain of life."

Daily Tonic

Water, Honey & Lemon

Ingredients
16 oz glass
Raw organic honey
Lemon
Apple cider vinegar (optional)

Directions
- Pour filtered water into a glass.

- Add one teaspoon of honey.

- Heat the mixture in the microwave
  for about 90 seconds.

- Stir to distribute the honey.

- Slice a lemon in half.

- Add a generous squeeze into the water.

- Stir.

Enjoy!

(You may substitute a teaspoon of apple cider vinegar for the lemon. If so, warm the water first before adding the vinegar.)

"I Love You"

Could these be the most powerful words on earth? Three little words. They could switch a mood, turn a life around, or change the world.

Say "I love you" as often as you can and as much as you can. Let the words flow off your tongue like beams from the sun. Make it so easy to say that it becomes as effortless as the breath you take.

Say "I love you" to the teenager who frustrates you, the spouse who adores you, and the parent who loves you deeply enough to set you free.

At the start of a discussion and the end of one, declare "I love you." Sometimes, playfully interject the words when there is a pause. It will add a sure smile to your companion's face.

Don't forget to tell yourself that you love you! It may sound strange at first, but practice doing it - in front of the mirror, when you're journaling, before falling asleep at night, and in the morning when you wake up.

Say it once, say it twice. Say it within, whisper it, and shout it out!

Loving Me

(All the little and big things you love about yourself.)

Hungry for Hugs

When was the last time you really hugged someone? A real hug is when you completely wrap your arms around the person, and you allow the person to do the same to you.

Hug someone long enough to inhale the sweet fragrance of perfume or the scent of freshly-washed hair. You don't move away immediately. You don't count the seconds.

Don't air-kiss. Offer a kiss on the cheek, or even two.

Pull back ever so slowly. Smile with your eyes. Let the person know that you're happy to see her.

If you're hugging your child, reach down towards him and lace his hands around your back. Then pull him as close as you can towards you. Stay hugging him until he releases his hold from you.

Play the "hug game" at home. Every time your loved one is about to pass you, stop, and exchange hugs.

Hugs

"My kids and I meet nightly in my son's bed.
We take turns sharing one thing for which we are thankful.
Sometimes, my children surprise me with their answers
but they never fail to share one.

'I'm thankful for my eyes. My IPad. My friends. Pizza.
For my blanket. For our hugs."

— Annie Singh-Quern

Kindness Reigns

Share a word or deed of kindness every day without expecting anything in return.

Something small, big, spontaneous, or planned.

Smile. Open a door. Pay a compliment. Pay it forward.

To a friend, a child, and a stranger. Watch their faces light up. See their spirits glow.

Share words of kindness as you would often utter the word, "I." Experience the bubbles of joy it brings to your day.

Compliment yourself.

"Always choose 'fabulous me' over 'flawed me.'"

— Annie Singh-Quern

Just Say "No"

Saying "yes" all the time can pull us away from our inner selves. On the other hand, learning to say "no" will give us more time to understand and care for ourselves. We can say "no" if our gut tells us so, if we are too busy, physically exhausted, or if the proposal takes us away from our loved ones. We should also say "no" to toxic situations and people.

The phone rings. It's your bestie. She has front row tickets to a favorite show. It's a work night, and you have a 10 pm bedtime, but the tickets are free, and she's your dear friend. Though it is tempting to accept the invite, it might be best to decline politely. However, let her know that you'll be happy to go for a walk one evening that suits both of you. You'll get your fitness in and spend quality time with your girlfriend.

How do you say "no"? Just say "no," or "no, thanks." Short and sweet.

Learn to say "no" firmly and without guilt.

Say "no" to unnecessary things, situations, events, and people, so you can spend more time connecting to you.

When to Say "No"

(... to people, things, and situations.)

Silence is Golden

Life is constantly pulling us in many directions. From the moment we step out of bed to the second before we close our eyes, we're always on the go. So much so that we forget to pause or stop, and then, at the end of the day, we are physically, mentally, and emotionally exhausted.

In the middle of a hectic day, come to a complete stop just by simply sitting. Don't plan it. Just halt in your tracks and sit. Not to watch TV, to eat, to chat on the phone, or fold laundry. Instead, sit because you deserve a break.

Maybe then, we can clear our minds, be inspired, hear ourselves breathe, and rest our weary heads.

If only we would sit.

Sitting

"When my daughter began walking at 14 months, we took strolls every morning to the park. In one corner was a circular path paved with "meditation" stones of brown, gray, and white. Olivia and I would lace fingers and tread slowly on the pebbles, barefooted. My girl's small, cushy soles seemed to contour perfectly with the smooth surfaces.

On a regular day, it took about five minutes to circle back to where our footwear lay. Sometimes, without any warning, Olivia would slip her small hand from mine and plop straight down on the path. Then, she'd looked up with a twinkle in her eyes, and a sweet smile on her face. She sat there for a long time just scanning her surroundings and playing with her toes. And I waited, mesmerized by how content she was - to just sit."

— Annie Singh-Quern

Make Music Your Muse

Music is food for the soul. It's an art and a language of sorts. It can also miraculously connect us to our inner selves and evoke emotions within us. It can motivate us, soothe us, make us cry, make us reflective, and make us want to dance.

Music genres:

- Jazz & Blues
- Classical
- Opera

During activities:

- Cooking
- Bathing
- Dining

Put on some music. Dance alone. Invite your loved ones to the dance floor.

Learn a dance, be it ballroom, modern, or another genre.

Play different songs from different music genres to evoke certain emotions, connect to your past and special people in your life, but remember to stow time during your day for silence.

Music & Musicians

(Songs and lyrics that pull at your heartstrings.)

Needs vs. Wants

Don't you wish we sometimes wore blinders when we are out shopping? That way, we would buy just what we need and not the countless items we want. Easier said than done!

If it's an outfit, make a pact with yourself to put your desires on hold for 48 hours. That extra time may provide you with enough strength to ask yourself if you really do want or need the item. Or, you may return home to find that you have something similar or better in your closet.

If you don't make the purchase, decide if there is a better way to use the funds. Could you save for that exotic family vacation next summer? You could also reward yourself for not making a purchase by putting the dollars in a safe spot for a rainy day.

If all else fails, stay away from the stores unless you need something specific. Or make a shopping list that you promise to follow. Or, put on your invisible blinders!

My Needs List

_____

_____

_____

_____

_____

_____

_____

_____

_____

_____

_____

(Experiences you need, and a plan to achieve them.)

Declutter & Detach

Pick up the first item in your home that you lay your eyes on. How much does it mean to you? Do you feel the object is in its rightful spot? If not, where does it belong? Asking these questions about things you surround yourself with will help you determine if they should be in your life.

Everything in our homes should have significance and they should sit in a meaningful place. Things that clutter our physical space may also cloud our minds. Decluttering allows us to open up our lives in many ways, physically, mentally, and spiritually. If you haven't used an item for a length of time, give yourself permission to consign, donate, or discard it.

Decluttering can be a physically daunting task to some homeowners, especially if there is much to sort through. If so, involve your family members to be a part of the activity. Tackle a room or a group of belongings, one at a time. Make a fun activity out of it.

When you detach and declutter, it may brighten up an area allowing you to see the surrounding items better and it may create room for something new. Decluttering will also allow you to feel lighter in body and mind.

Decluttering Plan

_____

_____

_____

_____

_____

_____

_____

_____

_____

_____

_____

(Areas in the home to declutter. Include schedule.)

Cash is King

Using only cash for purchases is a strict but very liberating way to manage your money. Not only does this kind of spending prevent you from indulging in impulsive purchases, but it may also curb your appetite for buying big unneeded items.

To get into the habit of taking only cash when you are out and about, decide on the amount of money to carry in your wallet. You can place yourself on a weekly cash budget or a monthly one. Make a promise that once the funds are exhausted, you won't be able to dig into the next month's stash until the time comes around.

Leave the credit cards at home if you plan to go shopping, especially if you think you may be tempted by all things lovely and new.

If you choose to go the cash route to make everyday purchases, you'll have fewer things in your home and more freedom in your life.

Monthly Budget

_____

_____

_____

_____

_____

_____

_____

_____

_____

_____

(Track a month of spending cash.)

Unplug

Separating ourselves from our electronics (phones, tablets, and computers) for certain periods enables us to carry out our daily lives more quietly and intentionally. Unplugging makes us feel as though we have more control over our days rather than being pulled constantly from one place to the next.

Concerned that you may be "missing out?" The longer you stay away from the dings of your phone, the more you will realize that you did not miss out on "important" happenings in the world. Instead, you may feel free and more connected to the people and things that mean the most to you.

Unplug your electronics for 15 minutes at least three to five times a day. Increase the frequency and length over time.

Disengage from your electronics during gatherings with a loved one, before tackling a mental task, and after a particular hour of the day.

Unplug Schedule

_____

_____

_____

_____

_____

_____

_____

_____

_____

_____

(Electronics to unplug various times of the day.)

Evening

Cook for Comfort

Cooking can be a very fulfilling activity. A memorable time in the kitchen does not require conjuring up an elaborate meal and setting out fancy dinnerware. Just enjoying the time and engaging all your senses preparing, cooking, and eating will be enough to make the experience special.

For those who prefer not to cook alone, invite a loved one to join you.

- Choose a healthy recipe.
- Buy or harvest fresh, organic ingredients.
- Preplan the meal and the division of chores.
- Soak in the magic show in the kitchen:
  - Burst of fragrances of cooked food.
  - Textures and shapes of diced vegetables.
  - Sizzle of hot oil; hissing of steam.
- Set the table with care.
- Light candles or turn down the overhead light.
- Eat slowly, savoring every bite.
- Engage in conversation that is deep and meaningful.

Spend time in the kitchen preparing and cooking a dish at least once a week.

Recipes

(New or favorite healthy dishes to try.)

Light a Candle

Have you noticed how a lit candle can instantly change the ambiance of a room and the mood of the people in it?

Turn off the overhead lights, the table lamps, and place the wall dimmers on pause. Then, light some candles.

Experiment with various scents, styles, and sizes - votive, pillar, and candelabra. Place candles on the dining room table, on the fireplace mantel, in your bedroom, and on your deck.

Soak in the magic of a candle at work - the silent dance of the flames, the clever shadows that seek the walls, and the softening of your loved ones' faces.

Dine by candlelight. Take a bath by candlelight. Share stories by candlelight.

Light candles frequently, but remember to extinguish them completely.

"If the single flame from a candle can melt the worries of the day away, what would a hundred flames do? "

— Annie Singh-Quern

Share Stories

One of the best ways to connect on a deep level with our loved ones is to share stories.

We can choose to turn the TV off, put our electronics away, and sit together just to chat.

Choose a place - the dining room table during dinner, in front of a glowing fire, or in the comfort of a bed, snuggling with your loved ones.

Think of a theme - funny stories, celebrating the legacy of a loved one who has passed away, or childhood days.

Listen. Ask questions. Seek details. Write the stories down, or store them in your memory bank.

Sharing stories is a beautiful way to treasure the past and the lives around it.

Stories

_____

_____

_____

_____

_____

_____

_____

_____

_____

_____

(Memorable stories - shared or for sharing.)

Shower Stress Away

Truly savoring a shower or bath should be an integral part of your self-care practice.

Begin your shower time by hanging a do-not-disturb sign outside the bathroom door. This is one of your sacred moments, and it's OK to let your loved ones know it.

Be picky with your pampering choices. Soft soap over hard? Fragrant or unscented? A washcloth or a loofah sponge? Music or candles, or both?

When taking a shower, adjust the showerhead to a massage or stream setting. Allow the water to run in rivulets, down your body. Feel the smoothness of your skin perfumed by the soap.

Allow ample time for the warmth to wash away the worries of the day. Let the anxiety and frustration slide right off you, and disappear in the drain beneath your feet.

To further enjoy your experience, select the right towel. Soft or fluffy? A relaxing shade of blue? Hang your towel outside the shower so you can reach for it easily without feeling a draft of cold air.

Begin a ritual of showering or taking a bath at any time of the day, just to unwind.

Bathtime Basket

(Assemble a basket of items for a relaxing bath.)

Scrumptious Shower Scrub

Oats, Honey & Yogurt

Ingredients
1/3 cup organic rolled oats
1 tbsp raw organic honey
1 tbsp plain yogurt
2 tbsp filtered water

Directions

- Pulse the oats in a food processor into a fine powder.
- In a small bowl, mix yogurt and honey.
- Let sit for two minutes.
- Add oats and stir.
- Allow the oats to absorb the yogurt-honey mixture for two minutes. It should transform into a paste (add a few extra drops of water, if necessary).
- Spoon the paste into a small jar.
- Smooth the scrub onto damp skin, using your fingers.
- Let sit for two minutes.
- Rinse.

(Use natural ingredients from your pantry, fridge, or garden to create your own scrumptious shower scrub. Always test a tiny amount on the inside of your wrist for any sensitivity.)

"Gratitude helps pave the path for meaningful days."

— Annie Singh-Quern

Gratitude

Practicing gratitude is a powerful way to live.

Choose a time during the day to write in your gratitude journal. List five things you're grateful for today.

You may start with the big things such as the sun and our health. Think of the little things too - the candle's flame that gives light to the room during a power outage and the rhythmic beating of our hearts that propel life-sustaining blood to trillions of cells. Even the pennies in our piggy banks add up to buy that carton of milk for our cereal, and tiny seals in our walls block the cold draft during harsh winter months.

Being thankful for the big and little things will help us live our lives feeling more fulfilled and peaceful.

Thankful for...

_____

_____

_____

_____

_____

_____

_____

_____

_____

_____

(... people, situations, and some things.)

Early to Bed, Early to Rise

Going to bed early allows you to rest and recharge fully for the next day.

Set a routine for an early bedtime. Schedule it in your calendar as you would any other appointment. Set an alarm or a timer, if necessary.

Move your muscles in the evening. Go for a walk or stretch lightly.

Eat dinner about three hours before bed. Refrain from snacking. Avoid caffeine.

Turn all electronics off about one hour before climbing into your bed.

Get excited about going to bed. Add soft music, a candle, a steamy shower or bath. Slide under fresh, clean sheets. Snuggle with a warm blanket. Read.

Give yourself at least eight hours of sleep.

Go to bed at the same time so you can get up at the scheduled time.

Bedtime Promise

Routine

_____

_____

Bedtime

_____

_____

Wake-up

_____

_____

(A routine for the best bedtime.)

Morning, Again

Breakfast in Bed

It's Sunday morning and you're awakened by the pitter-patter of rain. The sheets are toasty-warm and the curtains are drawn. You had a hectic week that ended on a high note. You've earned the right to sleep in. Indulge further - have breakfast in bed.

Accept the invitation from a loved one to make you breakfast. Or, prepare it on your own. A simple, delicious, and healthy choice should suffice. Arrange all breakfast items on a tray.

On your way back to bed, gather a small book or your diary.

Back in your room, place the tray on your bedside table, or bring it to bed with you.

Set the mood by opening the window shades to allow the beautiful rays in, light candles, or turn the side table lamp on.

Select soft music with or without lyrics. Or relax in silence. You may hear the sounds of nature calling outside your window.

Enjoy your breakfast, slowly and deliberately, savoring each bite. Feel free to pause, read, and write before returning to dining.

Give yourself permission to sleep in and enjoy breakfast in bed on a regular basis.

"We must make it a priority to carve out time in our day for self-care. If we don't care for ourselves, who will?"

— Annie Singh-Quern

Move Forward
& Stay Centered

Congratulations! You've completed the first steps to self-care!

If you have tried all of the practices, then great! If you were able to get through some of them, that's OK too. What's important is that you've taken steps to care for your inner self.

Now that you have engaged in self-care, let's talk about moving forward. What's your vision for self-care? Are there certain self-care practices that suit your lifestyle? Place these on the self-care vision board (next page) using a combination of writing, drawing, clippings from magazines, and printouts from your computer.

Keep "Journey into Simple Living" close to you (e.g., your sacred space) so you can view your vision board frequently. Is it time to include more self-care activities or increase the frequency of the ones you're practicing?

The key is to keep moving forward to stay centered and immerse yourself entirely in a simple living lifestyle.

Happy simple living!

Annie

Self-Care Vision Board

Notes

Notes

Self-Care Calendar *Week 1*

Monday

_____

_____

_____

Tuesday

_____

_____

_____

Wednesday

_____

_____

_____

Thursday

_____

_____

_____

Friday

_____

_____

_____

Saturday

_____

_____

_____

Sunday

_____

_____

_____

Goals for next week

_____

_____

_____

Self-Care Calendar *Week 2*

Monday

_____

_____

_____

Tuesday

_____

_____

_____

Wednesday

_____

_____

_____

Thursday

_____

_____

_____

Friday

_____

_____

_____

Saturday

_____

_____

_____

Sunday

_____

_____

_____

Goals for next week

_____

_____

_____

Self-Care Calendar *Week 3*

Monday

_____

_____

_____

Tuesday

_____

_____

_____

Wednesday

_____

_____

_____

Thursday

_____

_____

_____

Friday

_____

_____

_____

Saturday

_____

_____

_____

Sunday

_____

_____

_____

Goals for next week

_____

_____

_____

Self-Care Calendar *Week 4*

Monday

_____

_____

_____

Tuesday

_____

_____

_____

Wednesday

_____

_____

_____

Thursday

_____

_____

_____

Friday

_____

_____

_____

Saturday

_____

_____

_____

Sunday

_____

_____

_____

Goals for next week

_____

_____

_____

About the Author

Annie Singh-Quern's connection to the simple life began as a little girl growing up in Guyana. When she was just three years old, her parents moved to live in the rural parts of the country. She trailed after her dad during house visits to his patients' homes and grew to love the written word through her mom - a teacher, and an avid reader. In the summers, Ms. Singh visited her paternal grandparents in the country where the simple life reigned. Watching her grandfather light oil lamps before dusk and escorting him to the rice fields to milk the cows at dawn are some of her favorite childhood memories.

In 1983, at the age of 17, Ms. Singh-Quern moved to Minnesota to begin a new chapter in her life. In 2000, after graduate school, the author left the U.S. for new adventures in Singapore and Dubai, and became a mother of Olivia and Connor. During her stint overseas, Ms. Singh-Quern traveled throughout Asia and Europe. The simple life called to her once again - from the lush rice fields of Bali, Indonesia to the quiet waters of Phuket, Thailand. In 2013, the family moved back to the U.S. to settle in Peachtree City, Georgia, where the author now lives with her children.

Ms. Singh-Quern is the founder and CEO of *COA Consulting, LLC*, a marketing and communication agency, that serves small and medium-sized businesses.

She's the creator of *I AM Phenomenal Woman/Celebrate Greatness*, a platform that supports the personal and professional development of women. Here, regularly held pow wows, workshops, and annual events bring women together to communicate, celebrate, and collaborate their intrinsic greatness.

Ms. Singh-Quern can be reached by email (annie@anniequernconsult.com) or through her business website (coaconsultingservices.com).